Deeply Personal

A collection of poems & paintings to share with you

By

Rod Straw

First published 2023

Edited by Robin Fugill

British Library Cataloguing in Publication Data.

A catalogue record for this book is available from the British Library.

ISBN 978 0 86071 919 9

Front Cover Picture

St. Giles Church, Sandiacre, Derbyshire, from the Erewash Canal

Brief Church History

Courtesy of Wikipedia

The church dates from the 11th century. The chancel was added around 1342. The church was restored in 1855 and 1866. Further work was carried out in 1883, when new pews and a new organ were installed, new bells provided, and gas chandeliers added. The floor was laid with Minton encaustic tiles and the walls were stripped of plaster.

Contents

Poems Melancholy and Mindful

Foreword

Welcome to my book of poems which I have been writing over the years, usually inspired by some event and sometimes by sadness and grief, particularly at the loss of a close relative or friend.

My inspiration to publish this book has come from the generous comments of family and friends, who have read some of my poems, and have urged me to publish them. The ultimate motivation came from the choir in which I sing and help run, which held a concert in which one of my poems had its first public airing. Our choir's Musical Director, had very kindly put the words of 'An English Country Lane' to music and produced a beautiful video, and narrated the poem for me. The poem produced such an incredible wave of compliments and again comments like "have you written others" and "you should publish them".

Like all projects I've found they have highs and lows and I had reached a period of self-doubt and thought maybe writing poetry should just remain for personal enjoyment. However, my good friend Robin, during one of our regular coffee meets asked where I was with my plans to publish my poems. He rekindled my spirits and said he thought they were good enough, and not only re-energised my motivation but also offered to edit my book.

Many thanks Robin you are a true friend.

Notes from the Editor

Do you ever look back on life and wish you'd done, maybe not done, something? What would it be? Did you know that some of the most common regrets people have include, 'having taken better care of themselves' and 'to have done more for others.'

I have loads of things that I wished I'd done, or at least done better! Ranking up there in my league table of champion regrets is to have enjoyed poetry more at school. Actually, I loved school - unlike our author in *Too Young for School*! School was a social club, a drama group, sports team, great friendships! But, amidst all this fun, I utterly side-stepped its main purpose which was to teach me and to pass exams -aaarrghh! And within that aaarrghh of regret, is poetry. At school we read some great poets: MacNeice, Auden, Hopkins, McGough, Straw (oh no he came much later!). Skilled masters of the pen, who could capture imagery and, who I, between the ages of 11-19 failed to appreciate. If I was ever to write a poem, my first one should be entitled, *'Should Have Started School at 20!'*

I went to a university where a big name in poetry worked. He was the University Librarian. He turned down the position of Poet Laureate whilst I was still there! Most days, when in the library, I would see the man. His name was Phillip Larkin, and only much later did I realise how awesome that experience should have been, to stand in such proximity of a master.

As I grew, I realised that poetry isn't the difficult and inaccessible form that my brain said it was, but a stunningly efficient way of capturing life with an economy of words that every politician throughout time should have emulated. Poetry's ability to express profound experiences or events, and to do it in rhythm and rhyme, is not only clever but special.

In this book *Deeply Personal* we have a collection of experiences, witty, sad, moving, short, long, all telling of life seen through the eyes of its author and, which many of us can relate to. We all bask in nostalgia, face life's battles, observe the plight of others and here in this collection they remind and bring the story of life together in a focussed and lyrical way.

And what a wide range there is. From the joy of our climate through *The Cruel Wind, Glorious Golden Autumn* and *Bleak Winter Days* to the joy of our country when reading the evocative *English Country Lane* and the illustrative *Snowdonia and the Lleyn*- pronounced Thleen.

Then there's joy of family and friends seen in the *Bank Holiday Monday Bike Ride* and the *Life of Brian*. The humour of sport through the eyes of *The Tennis Ball* or the Oh so funny (if you ever tried to play it) *Lament of a Deranged Golfer*.

Enough! These just break the surface. There is sun and sadness in these pages. Read them for yourself and decide. Forget any past regrets and simply enjoy this journal of life.

Let me finish with words from the poem '*Deeply Personal*' because it sums up so well the treasure in the book and that poetry, to the reader, is itself 'deeply personal'.

Poems can serve like paintings,
Not pictures but richness of words,
That remind you of life's experience,
Thoughts of freedom just like birds.

Whatever these poems convey to you,
Perhaps your thoughts they'll help employ,
To transport you to a special place,
I truly hope you will enjoy.

Robin Fugill

In Aid of Muscular Dystrophy

Many of us, thankfully, get through life reasonably unscathed, but still a large number have the dreadful misfortune to contract a life limiting disease, which not only makes life very difficult for them, but also for their close relatives and carers.

Muscular Dystrophy is the cruellest of diseases, which progressively destroys normal human activities we all take for granted. It takes away personal mobility, to the point where a sufferer is unable to undertake the most necessary of functions unaided, and often requiring hoists to be lifted from their bed and to be taken to the bathroom; wheelchairs and mobility scooters providing the only way of escaping from the confinement of being permanently indoors.

Sadly within our own family, My Daughter-in-Law's and Son's nephew George was diagnosed with the Duchenne's form of Muscular Dystrophy at the age of four, following which his young life started to be deprived of a normal childhood. At eleven his life has become severely affected. George shows tremendous courage and determination every day. He attends a normal secondary school, where he is shown incredible support and kindness from his schoolmates.

Thanks to a generous sponsor, all the proceeds from sales of the book will go to the MD UK charity, which works tirelessly to research a preventative cure, and provide treatment to help sufferers deal with difficulties few of us can imagine.

Thanks for helping
Rod Straw

Deeply Personal

I composed these deeply personal poems,
My innermost thoughts within this book,
I invite you to share them whenever you wish,
Or maybe take an occasional look.

Will they conjure up fond memories?
Emotional moments in your life?
Hopefully you'll think of happy times,
Chase away periods of hurt and strife.

Whatever these poems may mean to you,
I hope they will help inspire your mind,
To reflect on those you love, or loved,
Those you may have lost or left behind.

Perhaps you will recall those special places,
Which mean so much within your heart?
And help you think of times of joy,
Not when your world seemed torn apart.

Poems can serve like paintings,
Though not pictures but richness of words,
That remind you of life's experience,
Thoughts of freedom just like birds.

Whatever these poems convey to you,
Perhaps your thoughts they'll help employ,
To transport you to a special place,
I truly hope you will enjoy.

The Cruel Wind

Relentlessly his ways to roam,
The cruel wind blows a fiendish tone,
Trees bow heads as if to please,
But still the cruel wind will not cease.

Tall grass parts at their master's will,
He passes on then all is still,
Still only for a second's breath,
A victim flower lies bent in death.

Has this cruel wind been sent from hell?
For by his wrath all nature fell,
Then dawn arrives, the wind abates,
Back to his lair, and there he waits.

'Til all is calm, and damage rent,
His anger soothed, his madness spent,
And so he rests now all is done,
His savage course once more to run.

An English Country Lane

It makes no difference where I am
Or wherever I may roam.
Sometimes it may be very near
Or far away from home,
But my treasured thoughts within my mind,
Always they remain,
To when I'm walking down
A beautiful, English country lane.

When anger seems to be trying
To tear the world apart,
And conflict's often evident
In many a person's heart,
At times like this I yearn for peace,
And my thoughts return again,
To when I am walking down
A beautiful, English country lane.

I often see the hedgerows
Embraced in colourful wildflowers,
Where birds are singing sweetly
Through glorious, daylight hours,
Young chicks in nests are snugly kept
In their cosy, safe domain,
Nestled in their avian home within
A beautiful, English country lane.

An English Country Lane....

Willow trees bow to their roots,
As if in permanent salute
To their earthly bounds to which
They seem to be so resolute.
Bright poppies, shining faces
In bright vermillion mass,
Greet me with a friendly wave,
As down the lane I pass.

Buzzing bees, flitting to and from
Each brightly coloured flower,
Industrious, yellow striped workers
Making the most of every hour,
With summer, just like clockwork,
The bees return here yet again
To the picturesque tranquillity of
A beautiful, English country lane.

If I could paint like Constable,
A picture I'd create
Of hedgerows, trees and flowers
And a wooden country gate.
When the modern, noisy world intrudes,
There's a place peace will remain,
It's around the timeless splendour of
A beautiful, English country lane.

Beautiful Spring

Spring arrives.
Now is the time for nature to renew.
Wispy clouds drift serenely by,
Over skies of azure blue,
Newborn lambs test spindly legs,
Leaping nimbly in the air,
Anxiously bleating with concern,
Seeking mother's tender care.

Grass starts making frantic growth,
As if it's trying to reach the sky,
Gardeners from their winters rest,
Have now to say goodbye,
And the weeds are sadly not exempt,
From spurts of growing intent,
It's time to fertilise the soil,
Lots of money to be spent.

Expectant springtime flowers
Striving, for their tiny buds to burst,
To ensure their vibrant coloured display,
Will be among the first,
Branches wave on bending trees,
As March winds make them list,
New leaves unfold at sun's command
In Early Morning mist.

Beautiful Spring....

In the countryside the new grass
Makes the pastures appear so lush,
Birds building nests to hatch their young
Seem always in a rush,
The honeybees and ladybirds
Become extremely active,
Warming sun wakes butterflies,
With wings stunningly attractive.

Springtime lifts people's spirits,
Washes away those winter blues,
Flowers drench the world in bright colour,
Lovely pastel shades and hues,
Spring imbibes much optimism,
As gladdened hearts abound,
Late spring heralds summer's arrival,
Longer days soon to be found.

Delightful Days of a British Summer

Delightful, British summer days,
Are totally unsurpassed,
Trees resplendent in full leaf,
And meadow flowers amassed,
Hills, vales, and pastures green,
Mop up the sun's warm rays,
Children play in fields and parks
On bountiful summer days.

The sun exalted in the sky,
Extend hours of light each day,
Folk can spend more time outdoors,
Enjoying picnics rest and play,
So many lovely places to visit
Within our evocative Isles
With many picturesque routes to follow,
Along many scenic miles.

The seaside acts as a magnet,
Attracting people to the coast,
Endless hours on sun kissed beaches,
Folks seem to love the most,
High reaching cliffs with incredible views,
Yielding numerous coastal walks,
Glistening seas, wide deep blue skies,
And perpetual seagull squawks.

Delightful Days of a British Summer....

A variety of picturesque landscapes,
Lie within our British shores,
Four countries each with unique charms
Are waiting to be yours,
Scotland's Highlands, England's Peaks
And wide East Anglian skies,
Wales' Snowdonia takes your breath away;
Ireland's lochs anoint your eyes.

These jewels of coast and countryside,
So unique and much admired,
Dwell within the Nation's hearts,
Some minds become inspired
To write poems, compose music,
Take photographs to record
The lushly pleasant British Isles,
In summer so adored.

If you feel that you are fortunate
To live within these sceptered Isles,
Forget rain and fog, or similar annoying guiles
Rarely is the weather extreme,
Despite the odd storm to contemplate,
Recall the delightful days of summer,
A good reason to call Britain great!

Glorious Golden Autumn

When autumn arrives, the evening sun
Fades sooner from the skies,
As each new day passes,
The sun's much later to arise,
It's clear for all to witness,
The decline from summer's heat,
Yet autumn has a unique charm
That many are pleased to greet

Moist morning air embraces ripened fruits,
Displayed in abundant number,
On trees' heavily laden boughs,
Ready soon for winter's slumber,
In summer they're adorned with leaves,
Of verdant, dancing greens,
But turning now, to reds and yellows,
Producing glorious, golden scenes.

Warm days give way to cooler air,
And the earlier encroaching night,
New dawns arrive with lower sun,
Saturating skies with golden light,
Mornings emerge with hedgerows
Draped in dreamlike, fairy lace
Of mist, distilled on spider's webs,
In this autumn's magical embrace.

Glorious Golden Autumn....

Autumn is a busy time,
For the industrious farming breed,
Collecting in the harvest,
Preparing fields for next year's seed,
The nights become much longer,
And days continue to recede,
Clocks fall back an hour,
In their diligent time keeping deed.

Lush autumn days, such uniqueness,
An exclusive, endless charm,
But Lower temperatures more likely,
Unlike summer's enfolding balm,
This season encourages many artists,
In their skilful, creative toils,
Capturing glorious, golden autumn,
Portrayed in water colours and oils.

As the days continue to shorten,
And harsh winter then arrives,
Spreading chilling winds, frost and snow,
Through everybody's lives,
The distant memories start to fade,
Of that beautiful golden dream,
Glorious golden autumn then takes flight,
With few traces of what has been.

Winter Days

Winter heralds in the drifting snows,
Cold northern winds and frost,
Crisp bountiful spring, long summer days,
Golden autumn, all now lost,
Just the thoughts of winter spoken,
Can bring us all a shiver,
Fear of floods, rains flowing from hills,
Fill up every brook and river.

But winter plays an important role,
In the balance of the earth,
Flora and fauna hibernate,
Storing vigour for spring's rebirth,
Hard frosts destroy those deadly bugs,
That threatens all plant life,
Whilst hardy plants, with frozen roots,
All battle to survive.

The welcome festival of Christmas,
Brings joy to shorter days,
Despite some loss of its true meaning,
It's still the birth of Christian ways,
The holiday time brings welcome rest,
For pressured working folk,
Time to enjoy their warming stoves,
Fuelled with yuletide logs of oak.

Winter Days....

The months of January and February,
Are sometimes difficult to contemplate,
As the rest of winter's weather,
Is what people seem to hate,
And these two months can sometimes yield,
The worst of winter's sting,
Snow and Ice, on dangerous roads,
Is what they often bring.

Boisterous March makes its presence felt,
Following on in winter's wake,
Strong gusty winds can blow down trees,
And branches often break,
But the days are gradually warming,
And the signs of spring are clear,
Time to move clocks on an hour,
Lighter mornings are now here.

April with its frequent showers,
Will be very soon arriving,
As winter moves to other climes,
And spring is on the horizon,
The sun now warming air and soil,
Rising higher in the sky
And the cold, chilling days of winter,
Are now thankfully saying goodbye.

The Tennis Ball

The yellow, spherical demon,
Flew like a bullet across the court,
From a wildly, wielded racquet,
But the service came to nought.

The tennis ball had little time
To recover all of its shape,
Cast aside for another ball,
He enjoyed a brief escape.

But soon our yellow victim,
Returned to the firing line,
When a fearsome overhead volley,
Destroyed his resting time.

There was little time to gather himself,
For the match was getting tense,
And the poor delirious tennis ball,
Had completely lost his sense.

Getting near the end of the set,
The game again reached deuce,
And the poor ball got little respite,
Whilst the players downed some juice.

It was back in play, with no warning at all,
The poor ball felt a sudden whack,
Immediately flying through the air again,
And another blow sent it back.

The Tennis Ball....

Thank goodness thought the tennis ball,
Resting briefly in a ball girl's hand,
Her skin was soft and gentle
And the feeling was quite grand.

Oh no, the player beckoned to the girl,
To throw him another ball,
And rapidly the ball returned in play,
Regretting his sudden recall.

It was reaching the end of the seventh game,
When suddenly the umpire bawls,
The score had reached four games to three
And it was now time for new balls

Hooray was the thought passing through the mind,
Of our little rotund friend,
It meant that his terrible, traumatic, time
Was coming to an end.

Whilst appearing in a final at Wimbledon,
Made him feel so very proud,
That's the end of my career on a tennis court,
The tennis ball avowed,

Then the ball was packed in a cardboard box,
And soon it fell asleep,
And whilst it travelled to another club,
The ball heard not a peep.

The Tennis Ball....

A few weeks passed and the ball relaxed,
In a warm club locker room,
Away from the constant whacks on the head,
And the inevitable, dreadful boom.

But little did he realise, the club
Had bought him as a championship ball,
And despite his recuperation
He soon would be back on call.

At the club's annual dinner,
The proud ball took centre stage
And whilst he should have enjoyed the attention,
Instead he flew into a rage.

Announcing the ball's fate,
He couldn't believe what the President said
"This ball was played in Murray's final"
With that the ball was whacked on the head.

Our battered friend, sick of being clobbered,
Felt enough was quite enough,
And thought it totally unreasonable,
To be treated quite so rough.

So a plan was hatching in his mind
And he feigned to feel unfit,
At match point in the president's game,
He pretended to develop a split.

The Tennis Ball....

The president he was furious;
He was expecting member's adoration,
But when he lost the match for the club,
He had only one explanation.

The ball had split, he protested,
And lost all its power and speed,
Just as he had the match sown up
And one point was his only need.

Loss of the match caused much discontent,
Resulting in a very long post-mortem,
The club secretary asked, why the president's shot,
Had been such a lousy short one.

The president complained it wasn't his fault,
He insisted the ball had developed a split,
The secretary's examination found the ball intact,
And he was having none of it.

The president had never been popular,
In fact he was a pompous bore,
And so having lost the club this match,
He was asked to play no more.
Furious no one believed him,
He descended into a raging fury,
He felt condemned without fair trial,
And sentenced lacking judge nor jury.

The Tennis Ball....

Now the club has a new president,
Who decided his predecessor's fall
Should be celebrated in great style,
With a glass case for the tennis ball.

So no longer will that tennis ball,
Be subjected to such great violence,
Instead he sits within the splendid honour,
In that illustrious showcase of silence.

So if you often play tennis,
And hit the ball with considerable ferocity
You may feel pleased, when you generate,
Such incredible, point winning velocity.

But spare a thought for the ball,
Don't be pompous, or show off to your mates,
For the ball may have the last laugh,
With feigned defects it generates.

The Fashion Genie's Out of the Bottle

The Fashion Genie's out of the bottle,
And the internet is running rife,
Some say social media has been a boon,
For others it's ruined their life.

Surely this technology was intended
To improve life for one and all?
But hasn't it just done the opposite?
With results that often appal?

Automatic telephones have to be endured,
Inviting you to press hash, one, two or three,
All we want is simply to speak to a human,
But that is so very unlikely.

You're in a queue; they're all very busy,
Due to a high level of calls on the line,
Then you're subjected to mindless, inane music,
For at least twenty minutes at a time.

Voices on televisions are far less clear
And local dialects seem to abound,
Dramas with actors lines so quietly spoken,
Means you have to keep turning up the sound.

The Fashion Genie's Out of the Bottle....

Is it just an age thing or has music
Taken a turn for the worse?
What on earth is this RAP thing all about?
There's no melody, tune or verse.

What inspired the trend of people,
To cover their skin with obscuring tattoos?
How will they look as their skin thins and wrinkles,
And the smoothness with age it'll lose?

Now so many men are sporting beards,
It seems like a fashion spreading thing,
When fashion has finally run its course,
What's the next fad that fashion will bring?

Decorating hasn't escaped from the fashion
Of copying programmes on television,
No longer individual colour schemes designed,
It's either grey or white the decision.

Where's all the independent thinkers gone?
What happened to creativity?
Instead of having individual thought,
Copying others is the dominant activity.

The Fashion Genie's Out of the Bottle....

Animals haven't been ignored by fashion,
Designer dogs have become the rage,
Curly coated poodles, mixed with other breeds,
Have now taken centre stage.

No more children propelling scooters with legs,
Relying on electric power to get around,
It applies to adults with expanding girths,
Exercise may help in losing the odd pound.

The Fashion Genie is out of the bottle,
And it's Unlikely it will ever go back in,
Life constantly changes beyond recognition,
But it puts some older folk into a spin.

Fond Summer Memories

Garden furniture is back in the shed,
Once bountiful rose flowers are now dead,
Bright blue skies being replaced by dark grey,
Fluffy white clouds slowly drifting away.

Five in the morning no longer sun bright,
Long warm evenings have now taken flight,
For the sun has now chosen to itself reposition,
Replaces our emotions with a changed disposition.

The lights now switched on no later than eight,
Soon, turning back clocks, will be time's fate,
A need to switch on the central heating,
And forget the pleasure of outdoor eating.

Of course surviving hot days with a blistering sun,
Isn't what we'd imagined as being much fun,
But our memories, we know, are very selective,
Only remembering our likes when being reflective.

Summer days are what most of us like the best,
We think of warm long ones and forget the rest,
We sink into autumn, fearing winter's dark sting,
Fond memories of summer to which we still cling.

The Old River Bridge

The deep river flows beneath your roof,
Reflects your face held high aloof,
Water dances round your piers of stone,
Whilst you sit upon your majestic throne.

For there you have been since time forgot,
Your life is simple, you need time not,
The rippling river is your only friend,
You welcome its water's then onwards send.

Neighbourly trees reach in fond embrace,
Nourished by the waters which past you race,
And here you have lived your simple life,
Untroubled by worries, stresses or strife.

If only you could tell of your remarkable birth,
About those who built you, their sorrows and mirth,
But your secret will always within you remain,
On your throne, on the river, over which you still reign.

Warm June Days of Wimbledon

The air is still and comfortably warm,
Long delightful June days of perfect form,
The thud of a tennis ball breaks the relative peace,
Wimbledon on the television, forms the centrepiece,

Through the open door drifts a gentle breeze,
Outside the sonorous hum of industrious bees,
I'm slouching lazily in the comfort of my chair,
Glued to the TV, as deuce point ball flies through the air.

June is the unpredictable star of the English summer,
Sometimes hot and unkind to the long distance runner,
Also to the tennis player, exposed to searing heat,
In a centre court battle, facing the prospect of defeat.

But for me with Pimms in hand, I'm devoid of any stress,
Until the player I'm banking on, gets into a dreadful mess,
Nothing I can do despite my very encouraging whims,
So I pour another glass, of delightful ice cool Pimms.

About My Paintings

I have to confess the idea to include paintings in a poetry book wasn't mine. Robin, who not only kindly agreed to edit my book, also suggested it would add variety and interest to feature a local amateur artist. Well I qualify on both counts.

It also sparked enthusiasm in me for another hobby of mine, painting pictures, as I've done over the years. Rather like my poetry writing. I should mention that the format of the paintings is not conducive to fitting on these pages. Hence some cropping was necessary including the spire on Truro Cathedral.

I have included some of my work, which started with my only attempt so far at an oil painting, of Truro Cathedral. The rest being water colours

I often wish I'd taken some art lessons as everything has been experimental for me. I do struggle a bit though with being logical sometimes, and when I get the bug, it's off to the shops, buy the paints and get cracking.

Perspective also seems to be a problem for me, and you will note some of my buildings have a bit of a tilt on, especially my watercolour of the Erewash Canal.

Painting however is very therapeutic and a great companion to another hobby of mine photography. I would encourage anyone who fancies trying either to give it a go. I've attached some notes about the paintings on the next two pages. Hope it prompts you to give it a try.

About My Paintings

'Daisies P32' This was my first attempt at a water colour and I was fairly happy with the result. I was, however, lucky to have been given a DVD on how to paint this picture.

This proves that a lesson, in whatever form, is the sensible approach to anything. The great thing about a DVD, although becoming old technology I guess, you can keep going back over and over anything if you lose the thread.

'Erewash Canal P33' I painted this from the front cover picture of this book, which includes St Giles Church, Sandiacre, Derbyshire.

The photograph is one I took on one of my many cycle rides along the Erewash Canal. It's very poignant for me for several reasons; firstly because my Mum and Dad were married there, and a few years later, WWII permitting, I was christened there in 1946. I was also a choir boy at St Giles too.

'Evan's Mill, Darley Abbey' P34 This delightful setting is on the River Derwent less than a mile from my home and a very familiar place. Again I photographed the setting and spent quite a lot of time trying to get the water realistic. There is a large weir where the main river rushes to join the lower level. To the side of this is a flood pound where the water is often gentle and mirror like. Getting the waters reasonably realistic was quite a challenge.

I've included a photograph of the same scene, page 35, to show how after a few years since I painted the picture, the trees have grown and partially masked the scene.

About My Paintings

'Everything's Seems Blue P36' On the back of the painting of daisies, I was tempted to waver from the traditional to the more surreal, but only slightly. I was happy with the result until someone said does it look like a piece of wallpaper? Who needs friends anyway?

'St Edmund's Church P37' Another local scene, again close to home on St Edmund's Close, at the heart of the original Allestree Village and next to the Red Cow public House.

This was painted also from a photograph which I enlarged and drew on it a grid to get the scale and proportions as close as I was able.

'A Stormy Day at the Sea Shore' P38 This was also a tutorial on the same DVD as the daisies painting. There are a couple more on it I will have a bash at one day. Maybe when I'm older and no longer cycling and motor cycling.

'Truro Cathedral P39' I painted this quite a while back when I was off work with mumps, to distract me from the boredom and pain. It is my favourite so far. I much prefer oil paints as the colours are much more dense and vibrant. I painted this from a historical postcard and it was the scene supposedly in the 17th Century. If you look on the cathedral website there is a photo from a similar position and it does look similar.

I hope this has been a pleasant break from the poetry. Maybe you think "I could have a go at water or oil painting". Perhaps you already do, and think you can do much better. I know many people can, but just don't tell me please. I'm happy in my own little world.

Daisies

The Erewash Canal, Sandiacre, Derbyshire

Evan's Mill, Darley Abbey, Derby

Photograph of Evan's Mill, Darley Abbey –
A few years on from my painting, hence more trees

Everything Seems Blue

St Edmund's Church, Allestree, Derby

A Stormy Day at the Sea Shore

Truro Cathedral in the Middle Ages

When Everything's Gone Quiet

It was a gradual, uncaring quietness,
That slowly took away the sound
Of my hearing a blackbird singing,
And trodden footsteps on the ground,
It wasn't me couldn't hear I thought,
Others are speaking far too low,
I questioned almost every word,
My comprehension far too slow.

I couldn't understand why the television,
Seemed to have lost its audible sound,
No longer words distinctly pronounced
In any programme could be found,
And what's that buzzing in my ears,
Sounds like someone's fired a gun,
At times it dominates my world,
But, they say nothing can be done.

An inner calm descends my mind,
As I let the loss of hearing dominate,
Then the tinnitus takes over the quietness,
With a ringing in my ears, which I hate,
Without my hearing aids it's impossible
To make sense of the multitudes of sound,
And the cacophony of noises and voices
Amidst the clamour of life all around.

When Everything's Gone Quiet....

My hearing is unlikely to improve,
In fact I'm told it may get worse,
So my antidote for this deafness,
Is composing my inner thoughts in verse,
I often think of other people's problems,
Far worse than being in my quiet dome,
Of the many people very ill in hospital,
Whilst I'm comfortable here at home.

It's so easy to feel sorry for yourself,
And to muse about your personal plight,
But not hearing so well as you get older,
Isn't the trauma, of maybe losing your sight,
And whilst I wouldn't recommend deafness,
Put your fingers in both ears to try it,
Now you'll discover what it's like
When everything's gone quiet.

The Antique Vienna Clock

The antique clock's heart constantly beats,
It has through the world's most memorable feats,
Splendidly suspended on the dining room wall,
For two centuries it's ticked away through them all.

As years pass it's asks little of its master,
Just help in making it go slower or faster,
Raising its weights and adjusting the pendulum,
Maintaining accuracy of this simple time engine.

The clock just requires an occasional clean,
On its workings a drop of light oil,
Then for many years this steadfast machine,
Will keep on with its time keeping toil.

One weight provides the time display drive,
The other one makes the clock seem alive,
Day and night it records the time,
Each hour and the half, a melodious chime.

It's simple, requires no battery,
No mains power or electrical circuit,
The clock is ecologically friendly,
Leaves no trace of carbon waste surfeit.

The Antique Vienna Clock....

Through generations and millions of lives,
Rhythmically ticking during their lives and demise,
With tender care and if kept fully wound,
It records the time with a delightful sound.

The devoted clock's kept on diligently ticking,
Through wars and many landmark events,
In its life it's rarely seen quitting,
Recording time from which it rarely relents.

Trying to Find Peace and Quiet

Trying to find peace and quiet these days
Is definitely no easy task,
Seeking uncrowded, quiet places,
Seems far too much to ask,
There's lots of noise everywhere,
In the air and on the ground,
Planes, cars, trucks and buses
In fact there's noise all around.

Wondering where I might find
The quiet calm I often crave,
I sought somewhere peaceful,
My Sanity perhaps I'd save,
Deciding to take our camper van
To lovely Henley on Thames,
I hoped I'd discover tranquillity,
In one of England's riverside gems.

My research was lax, my plan to find
Peace and quiet sadly back-fired,
A busy road next to the camp
Spoiled the peace that I desired,
And hadn't noticed on the map,
The proximity of noisy Heathrow,
The constant roar of planes overhead
That the campsite guide didn't show.

Trying to Find Peace and Quiet....

The leisurely stroll into Henley
Wasn't the hoped for Country walk,
But down a noisy main road,
And I could hardly hear myself talk,
Britain's increasing traffic volume
Seems a very disconcerting trend,
I keep on asking myself the question
Where On earth will it all end?

I confess in the past I've played my part
In increasing traffic and congestion,
After 40 years in the motor industry,
It's impossible to refute the suggestion,
But we all desire independent travel,
To go wherever and when we like,
But now I'm trying to do my bit
Travelling wherever I can by bike.

But it seems unlikely most of us,
Will give up on owning our cars,
Unless of course we ruin planet Earth
And maybe have to move to Mars,
So I guess we'll put up with the traffic,
Even if it's all electrically driven,
Intending to help stop polluting the earth,
We are fortunate to have been given

Bank Holiday Sunday Bike Ride with the Grandchildren

Early Bank Holiday Sunday, such a bright
Morning as we ventured outside,
Wheeling our bikes through the
Garden gate, to set off for a family ride,
The sun was creeping higher in the sky,
So blue right to the horizon,
Slumber slowly faded from our eyes,
And our spirits began to enliven.

Through the suburban streets we pedalled,
Not too fast for Max is not quite seven,
Harry pedalled with a bit more vigour,
But he's a year and half from eleven,
We passed by houses of varying styles,
Mostly from the early nineteen thirties,
Gardens filled with springtime flowers,
With shrubs and plants and trees with berries.

These silent roads in two days hence
Would then be full of heavy traffic,
Folk would be dashing to their work,
And the change would be dramatic,
As we progressed towards the Thames
Into view came Hampton Court
We agreed our cycle ride should be
A day full of fun and sport.

Bank Holiday Sunday Bike Ride....

The waters of the majestic Thames,
Were dappled by the early morning sun,
Suggesting a delightful bike ride ahead,
Which had only just begun,
Our destination for this riverside ride,
Was the Anglers at Teddington Lock,
Welcome refreshments we there consumed,
Replacing severely flagging energy stock.

The homeward journey saw more traffic,
On each road and busy urban street,
Delightful scenery of the Thameside landscape
Was now a forgotten treat,
Heaving our bikes over a railway bridge,
Seemed a worthwhile, shorter route,
But when we'd carried all six over,
We didn't feel quite so astute

The penultimate leg through Bushy Park,
Another lovely scenic jewel,
Coaxing Max to keep tired legs pedalling,
Almost seemed to be quite cruel,
But Hampton Court was ahead again,
The homeward straight was now in sight
And once recovered, both Harry and Max,
Agreed the day had been a delight.

With lunch consumed, a drink enjoyed,
We all were full of laughs and smiles,
Glancing at my bike's milometer,
We'd covered ten point seven miles
Recounting the ride through leafy suburbs,
And by the majestic River Thames,
We agreed, cycling England's pleasant land,
Is one of life's most wonderful Gems.

Bank Holiday Monday Bike Ride

(With the same Grandchildren)

Unlike our Sunday bike ride,
Monday had promised some rain,
We'd hoped to ride in bright sunshine
And get back home in the dry again,
But optimism is not an exact science,
And guesswork has so little power,
No sooner had we ventured forth,
We got drenched by a sudden shower.

The clouds flurried across a troubled sky,
And the sun came out again,
We were hopeful we'd not be troubled
By any further annoying rain,
The route we took was mainly
Narrow footpaths, unlike Sunday's ride,
At times the going was pretty tough,
Along paths we'd never before tried.

Through fields and over several styles,
We came to the gentle River Ember,
Flowing sedately towards the Thames,
A view we'd always fondly remember,
But our way was then completely blocked,
By a high fenced, caravan site,
It was turn back, or ride a narrow path,
The only options to our plight.

Bank Holiday Monday Bike Ride....

Decision made we used the route,
With lots of nettles so overgrown,
Where we soon heard poor Harry,
Let out a troubled, urgent, groan,
He'd toppled sideways from his bike
Right into a bed of nettles,
Searching for docks to sooth his stings,
We could only find dandelion petals.

Harry was brave, despite a lot of pain,
And soon back astride his bike,
We turned back from the nettle path,
As there was nothing there to like,
The only other choice for us,
Was to go through a large estate,
Preferring to have a countryside ride,
This route we just didn't rate.

The clouds were rolling in again as we
Pedalled down an urban road,
Harry and Max on the pavement,
But still observing a safe riding Code,
The pavements were uneven, caused by
Tree roots forming bulges and cracks,
Suddenly hitting one of these bumps
It sadly toppled poor little Max.

Bank Holiday Monday Bike Ride....

Max lost control, tumbled from his bike,
Hitting the ground with a sickening crunch,
So loud it disturbed a nearby resident,
Quietly sitting eating her lunch,
She offered kind assistance,
As we wiped blood from his Knee,
We told him to be brave, not cry,
The lady we assured how well he'd be.

This had been an eventful ride and in
Sharp contrast with Sunday's trip out,
But the beauty of cycling is in variety
And being tough is what it's about,
Harry and Max proved how brave they were,
Fighting back their pain and tears,
With punishing bike rides to look forward to,
Over the many forthcoming years.

Eventually, back at home, the promise
Of a deliciously welcome lunch,
Harry's memory of stinging legs fading,
And Max's hitting the ground with a crunch,
Perhaps this was not the ride we'd envisaged,
Coping with the vagaries of British weather,
But it still remains so very enjoyable,
For our family to go cycling together.

Better still if they are all in one piece at the end!

The Humble Bicycle

The freedom of the highways
For which we cyclists deeply care,
The pleasure of the byways
They remain beyond compare,
To pedal into freedom,
On our trusty, simple bike,
Transports us into miles of fun
Viewing scenes we so much like.

The bicycle protects the environment,
And takes little from the Earth,
It does not pollute the air we breathe,
It repays many times its worth,
The bike reduces traffic jams,
Takes little highway space,
The bike does not wear out the roads
As do cars and trucks with haste.

A more healthy way of low cost travel
Is impossible to find,
It helps tune up the body and is
Good for a well balanced mind,
So if the weather turns out fine
And you feel you're at a loss,
Take out your bicycle for a spin,
Who knows what you'll come across?

The Humble Bicycle....

Perhaps it's years since you rode a bike,
So long you've never thought to try,
Well maybe it's time to have a go,
Not let your chances pass you by,
Think you are out of condition?
May struggle to stand the pace?
Ride on a gentle, quiet road,
And don't attempt to race.

It's likely you'll get out of breath,
Your bottom may complain,
But the more you ride the better you'll feel
And the less will be the posterior pain,
As fitness improves and muscles build
And strength flows to your feet,
You may increase the journey lengths,
And who knows in races compete.

So much pleasure's gained from a Bike
And it's really worth a go,
It could be life changing in so many ways,
Of which you may not presently know,
You may decide to ride to work
And find free transport quite desirable,
Or if retired just ride for fun,
On that remarkable, humble, bicycle.

The Shock of the Old Man in the Shop Window

Yesterday walking past a shop window,
I looked at the reflection in the glass,
There appeared an old man at my side,
So I walked faster the old man to pass.

Gazing sideways at the next window,
Expecting to be walking on my own,
I couldn't believe that wasn't the case,
And it seemed I still wasn't alone.

Walking even faster I thought the answer,
At the next window I was hoping to see,
The old man appearing way behind,
But to my horror the reflection was me.

Too Young for School

Does anyone else think that it's unfair?
And my mother didn't seem to care,
To make a very young child start at school,
So I hatched a plan to act the fool.

The first morning I loudly bellowed and cried,
Ineffective, I lay still, hoping she'd think I'd died,
Wise to my antics, failing to have any desired effect,
With a swift grasp Mother soon had me standing erect.

On the way to school we passed many a child,
They all seemed calm and some quite mild,
My mother asked "Why can't you be bright and happy"?
I said "Give me a chance I'm only just out of a nappy!"

I dragged my heels and made such a noise,
Mum pulled me to school and said "Follow those boys",
I refused and yelled, the headmistress saw the battle,
And came to Mother's aid so I continued my loud prattle.

The headmistress, Miss Cole, grabbed me by the arm,
And tried through the fracas to apply some calm,
But it didn't work; I cried "I'm only four and a half"
Then let fly with a kick aimed at Miss Cole's left calf.

Eventually I was dragged to Miss Henderson's class,
Through the opened door I saw kids in a mass,
Of desks and bright faces, quietly sitting down,
I said "I'll sit with the black lad,"
His name was Keith Brown.

Too Young for School....

Keith was the only black child in the whole school,
And he had no option but to sit with this fool,
We became close friends and had masses of fun,
Firing loud banging caps behind adults from a gun!

My mother arrived home a complete mental wreck,
To make sure I'd not escaped she returned just to check,
As she peered through the railings during play time,
Relieved from the stress, she saw I was just fine.

In Dreams

I was the skipper of an ocean going yacht,
Sailed seven seas, cruised each foreign shore,
Hanging over the side, sun drenched and hot,
I awoke from a dream on the floor.

As a fighter pilot I screamed across the sky,
With a barrel role and vertical climb,
But I've never had a chance to fly,
I awoke from a dream at breakfast time.

In a studio recording my latest hit,
Another number one to make me a mint,
Singing in my sleep, I'd bitten my lip,
I awoke from a dream, finding I was skint.

I was stressing, a tricky time ahead,
As a distinguished surgeon things could go bad,
Thank goodness the patient wasn't dead,
I awoke from a dream, and I was glad.

I was on TV in a leading part,
My dreams were getting out of control,
Yet another Oscar winner on the chart
Was I dreaming or going round the pole?

Concerned that my dreams seemed risky,
A change of routine was clearly just right,
I missed out the several glasses of whiskey,
I was pleased not to dream again last night.

The Dissenting Voice of Reason

Being reasonable doesn't always make sense,
When those around you disagree,
Situations that make you feel tense,
When your point of view they fail to see.

Being reasonable doesn't always make sense,
If those around you aren't likeminded,
You may wish to mount a strong defence,
But sense and reason can often be blinded.

Being reasonable doesn't always make sense,
When you're trying to make a point,
But those you're attempting to convince,
Your sense of reason they try to disjoint.

Being reasonable doesn't always make sense,
It's not restricted to a particular season,
But bigotry can sometimes blind commonsense,
It's just the Dissenting Voice of Reason.

To Welcome the Sun Drenched Morn

Welcome to the sun drenched morn,
You've not been around for a while,
The rains and winds we dislike and scorn,
When you come out you make us smile.

Each morn when the sun comes out to stay,
It really brightens up our mood,
A better way to start the day,
Reducing any tendency to brood.

Of course we know the rain is vital,
But does it ever know when to stop,
Foreboding clouds means there is a sky full,
For farmers it can damage a vital crop.

The Aztec's had an inspired idea,
Worshiping the Sun from dusk till dawn,
They awoke each day without fail or fear,
To Welcome in the Sun Drenched Morn.

He is the Creator of Life

He is the light that arrives every morning,
He is the darkness that heralds in each night,
He is the Creator of storms without warning,
He is the Creator of good, so evil takes fright.

He is the maker of trees that are lungs of the earth,
He is the maker of water that fills oceans and seas,
He is the Creator of life, its death and birth,
He is the Creator of winds and the cool gentle breeze.

He is the Creator of food for the world's many nations,
He is Creator of love for every husband and wife,
He is the Creator of the world's populations.
'He is the Creator of Life'.

The Life of Brian

This ode is to my very good friend, I know as good ode Brian,
It seems as if when he was young, he was as strong as iron,
A tennis player of high repute, an admired svelte golfing champ,
But now just plays his saxophone, and moans about his cramp.

Surely nobody thinks that Brian, could really be over the hill,
There must be some useful life within, this former athlete still,
He's down life's road a way, and reached three score and ten,
He's still a fitter example, than many seventy year old men.

His knees may be getting dodgy and his back may often creak,
His sight is gradually fading, and his hearing is getting weak,
But when we go out hiking, he'll cover many a rugged mile
With no word of complaint, that is, until we come upon a style.

Surmounting Derbyshire's many dry stone walls,
His wonky knee gives way as he nearly falls,
His deft use of a walking pole, preventing disaster,
At Pirouetting over the wall he's become a master.

Sometimes we cycle, instead of going for a hike,
Brian then wheels out his shining, Boardman bike,
Often a walking buddy and a cycling companion,
With more oil on his chain than leaked from the Torrey Canyon.

We take sandwiches, coffee, biscuits and cake,
And stop for our lunch by a river, canal or lake,
Some may think this is no fitness programme,
They're correct, but we really don't give a damn.

The Life of Brian....

We are septuagenarians and we have lots of fun,
Walking and cycling, but we can no longer run,
We solve the world's problems, which always exist,
On the way home, at the pub, we practice Brahms & Liszt.

Though this ode may be lacking, in concise, measured brevity,
It was intended to say Brian, well done for making seventy,
Worry not if you often feel like a creaking gate,
Though you're an OAP, your mates still think you're great.

Secrets of the Skies

I sat beside the sea last night
And watched the moon fall out of sight,
I came again at break of day
To watch the early sun's display.

I often watch the sky at night
To wonder at the stars so bright,
And think if heaven's there somewhere,
How do departed souls get there?

The clouded skies hide each bright star,
Then clouds don't care what view they mar,
But twilight's clouds still play a part,
Those deep blue skies make works of art.

Do skies hide angels, or some dark fiend?
Can rainbow's end ever be gleaned?
Whatever earth's roof has on show,
Does it hold the secret of where souls go?

Snowdonia and the Lleyn

Sights that greet my appreciative eyes,
Are wondrous mountains rising up to the skies,
With deep valley streams advancing to be,
Sun spangled torrents rushing down to the sea.

Incredible vistas, there for all to see,
The stern granite crags and loose sliding scree,
Dense wooded hillsides of vibrant green,
Transfix one's eyes on views beautifully serene.

Rugged landscape gives way to a spectacular scene
The beautiful peninsula known as the Lleyn,
Surrounded by golden sands, and many a proud cliff,
Protesting against westerly's, blowing blustery and stiff.

This beautiful landscape so varied and wild,
Drenched by bright sunlight, appears peaceful and mild,
Yet when storms descend with ferocity and might,
This calm, tranquil beauty appears to take flight.

I will gladly return to this amazing land,
Of mountains and coastline, so majestic and grand,
Sun kissed landscape, high peak, valley stream
Forever I'll be in awe, of Snowdonia and the Lleyn.

(**Please note:** I wrote this understanding that Lleyn in Welsh is pronounced Thleen)

The Lonely Man at Grey's Court

(A National Trust House and Park)

The old man sat alone and unnoticed,
By the many people who were passing by,
He was looking quite sad and mournful,
And I couldn't help but wonder why,
His sandwiches appeared to be roughly made,
They seemed to be lacking a caring hand,
He had well-worn clothing and unruly hair,
And his skin was quite weathered and tanned.

The sun was high in the clear blue sky,
He'd sought shade from a large Beech tree,
Then from his battered, weathered bag,
He took a flask and poured a cup of tea
A solitary figure at the picnic table,
Which could have easily seated a family,
His demeanour gave an impression,
He may have been sad and perhaps lonely.

Among groups of people enjoying their day
He looked isolated and out of place,
There appeared little sign of happiness
In his deeply lined, solemn face,
Having finished lunch, he packed his bag,
And with an effort rose from his seat,
He walked away with faltering steps,
His respite appearing to be complete.

The Lonely Man at Grey's Court....

There must be many people living alone,
With a sad and broken heart,
It's possible this man was one them,
With a life that's been torn apart,
Or maybe he had a wife at home,
Said this wasn't where she'd wanted to go,
It's quite feasible he wasn't lonely at all,
But I guess I will never know.

For the Love of the Inland Waterways

The silver thread of water tempting
Discovery as it fades from view,
Inviting boaters to travel its waters,
Provides home for much of wildlife too,
Man made industrial highways,
Connecting distant port and shore,
In the past canals became abandoned,
Now attract leisure seekers by the score.

To cruise the canals and rivers
Of these splendid British Isles,
Is a unique, unequalled experience,
Creating everlasting smiles;
Boaters see familiar landscapes,
From an unfamiliar perspective,
Creates memories of pleasant times,
Often emotionally reflective.

There's so much varied wildlife
Inhabiting this evocative, watery world,
Swans, unperturbed, glide serenely by
Soaking up sun with wings unfurled;
Ducks swim along with their little chicks,
Trying to keep up with Mum and Dad,
Whilst tiny, swiftly, darting Coots,
Find so much pleasure can be had.

For the Love of the Inland Waterways....

These delightful landscapes passing,
At a leisurely four miles an hour,
Could be straight from a classic painting,
Though at times may seem a little dour,
As sprawling towns and cities draw near,
The tranquil scene will see a change,
That's the charm of cruising the waterways,
The constantly changing vista range.

But then a welcome halt in pace,
Can be enjoyed by encountering a lock,
First experiences of the change in levels,
Can sometimes be quite a shock,
Much effort can be required to
Open a heavy, hand wound sluice,
Filling and emptying deep locks can be
Rewarded by a drink of ice cold juice.

You can rest along miles of waterways,
You may decide to moor for the night,
Mooring next to the towpath,
Provides a tranquil evening of delight,
To find escape from the frantic strain,
Of what may feel like pressured time,
Waterways can chase those blues away,
With a pleasure quite sublime.

Lament of a Deranged Golfer

To think that this new golfer,
Expected the Game to be so much fun,
To hit a ball with a metal club,
Like it was being blasted from a gun,
Ignoring advice about the lessons
He really should have had,
His attempts always to hit the ball
Were understandably very bad.

The golfer bought expensive clubs,
A full set of shiny Pings,
He expected that he could definitely
Produce first class drives and swings,
But in his clumsy hands each Ping
Was nothing like a top class club,
He should have stuck to playing darts,
With his mates at the local pub.

After thrashing round the course,
And shifting loads of soil and turf,
The only thing he'd achieved was
Piling up lots and lots of earth,
The ball had hardly moved at all,
The small amount it did was the waft
Of the swirling, swinging Ping driver
And the rapid down force draft.

Lament of a Deranged Golfer....

Disillusioned, he realised he should have had,
Those advised lessons of golf tuition,
But intending to ring a local golf pro,
By mistake rang a psychiatric institution,
He should have put his glasses on,
To read the number in the directory,
To explain the problems he was having
With his very poor golf ball trajectory.

Resulting from his myopic error,
Having rung the Psychiatric institution,
He explained his serious state of mind,
And his considerable disillusion,
He confessed how much he had spent
On clothes and very expensive clubs,
And all he'd achieved was slicing
His golf balls, into adjacent woods.

The receiver of his call appeared
To be extremely kind,
Said he'd definitely rung the right place,
For a solution to his ills they'd find,
She said we have many people in here,
Feeling very much the same,
Who had also spent a fortune on what
Appeared to be a ridiculous game.

Lament of a Deranged Golfer....

She said no one in their right mind, would
Trudge six and a half miles around a field,
Amidst hard, white flying balls,
Without a hard protective shield,
She admitted that some of their patients
Had been hit by balls on the head,
By other golfers with no apology given,
Just shouting 'fore' for some reason instead.

So the golfer decided that having heard
Such an understanding tone,
This was just the place for him,
He would definitely feel at home,
So off he trotted, with clubs and balls,
Credit card and lots of lolly,
The staff confirmed He was without doubt
Most definitely off his trolley.

After three weeks in the place,
Among others quite deranged,
The golfer was looking forward
To games with patients he'd arranged,
He was the only one with any clubs,
His brand new top class pings,
The inmates said that with his clubs,
Their balls would fly with wings.

Lament of a Deranged Golfer....

The place was full of golfers
Who were also mentally disturbed,
Who had Left their wives at home
Feeling really, seriously perturbed,
With household budgets broken,
All under severe financial strains,
Since their spouses too, had taken up
This most ridiculous of pointless games.

But now the golfer is under control,
And supplied with a very special jacket,
Its canvass, it has buckles and straps,
To prevent him spending another packet,
Inside his softly, padded room,
He swings each club to his heart's delight,
With his carbon shafted golf clubs,
Smashing his golf balls out of sight.

"It's a Shame I Didn't Spend More Time at Work"

Don't assume that life's always fair,
Nor if you fail that someone else will care,
Self pity is rarely any kind of gain,
But may simply add to more strife and pain.

At times the trials of life can be tough,
In a world where effort is not always enough,
Where there's pressure to beat an exacting target,
Understanding for failure you're unlikely to get.

You may be encouraged to follow a more positive life,
Ignore that you're suffering from stress and strife,
And if victory comes by any devious measures,
Don't trouble your conscience, just take the pleasures.

But surely there must be a better way to live,
Not win at all costs, or to take and not give,
What would the world be like without compassion?
That human emotion not always in fashion.

Amidst the hectic pace of modern living,
There remains a fitting place for loving and giving,
If it's only time to share with someone's grief,
Expressed in their tears, may bring them relief.

So maybe it's worth finding a balance,
Between life outside of the chance,
Of climbing a ladder of profit and gain,
With reward and lots of emotional pain.

It's a Shame I Didn't Spend More Time at Work....

It's true life is not always fair or fine,
Nor do we always give our dear ones time,
To say how much we love and really care,
For that special person whose always been there.

As we approach the end of our life here on earth,
It's unlikely we'll say with any pleasure or mirth,
"I should have forsaken all others", then add with a smirk,
"It's a shame I didn't spend more time at work."

Melancholy and Mindful

This section I have devoted to mindfulness and to times of sadness, both personal and for us all, within our often turbulent world. I would hope they may help bring you some peace and comfort if you feel, or have felt, sadness or loss. If they are nothing more than just poems, I hope you still enjoy them.

I have also included poems inspired by moments of grief, not only for me but for relatives and friends no longer here, and for their nearest and dearest, who have experienced the pain of losing a close relative or friend.

Five poems I wrote for close friends at their funerals, and at times of loss in my own family. I have included as footnotes, a brief tribute to the person or persons concerned.

A few poems have a religious connotation, and as a Christian they have a bias to my own beliefs, but I hope whatever your personal beliefs may be, towards a spiritual and divine guidance for us in this world, you can share in some moments of peaceful reflection and introspection.

I gave the title to this book of poems 'Deeply Personal' and I hope it doesn't seem too self indulgent. I think poetry is a personal expression of many emotions, and the greatest joy is being able to share them with others.

But we must always find time to laugh, keep a sense of humour, and not be serious all the time.

Our Forefathers Fought So Bravely

Our forefather's fought so bravely to
Restore the world they hoped to save,
Their sacrifice for lasting peace
Went with them to their grave.

They surely never could have realised,
Senseless war would remain a scourge,
Nor could they have ever anticipated,
Violent dictators would re-emerge.

When past wars eventually come to an end,
With such a needless loss of life,
Returning to a normal existence
Always came at such a dreadful price.

Decades pass before economies recover,
Homes, hospitals, factories, all destroyed,
Many a dead soldier son mourned by his family,
Thousands left dead, starving, unemployed.

Why this senseless damage and destruction?
Why this continuous loss of peace?
Will the war mongers ever lose their blood lust?
Will their lack of compassion ever cease?

Weep Not For Me For I Am Free

Weep not for me for I am free,
I'm now at peace for eternity,
My earthly bonds I now release,
And rest within eternal peace.

The pain has gone, no more will come,
My battle is fought, my trial is done,
So I go now where my spirit can dwell
Around those I love and know so well.

It's not in the sky where I am found,
Nor in the earth below the ground,
Nor in the fields of childhood days,
Nor in the woods and country ways.

For I am now in all of these
And ride upon the gentle breeze,
So when I brush against your cheek
You'll know it's just how my spirit can speak.

Dedicated in loving memory of Sue Jones who sadly died on 12th August 2016. After the bravest of battles against an incurable and aggressive brain tumour from which she knew she would not survive.

Also my lovely Sister-in Law Pat Hills, who along with problems of old age, was finally diagnosed with liver and lung cancer which hastened her death at 87 years on 23rd July 2023.

Goodbye to Our Sailor

As the sun sank on the horizon and
Our sailor came to journey's end,
The dimming light of the final sunset,
Marked the passing of a shipmate and friend,
The treasured life with all its adventures
Of oceans and each foreign shore,
Came to its final conclusion, and our
Sailor slipped through life's open door.

We will remember his life as a sailor,
By the many ships on which he served,
Their names on the badges he displayed with pride
No more than our sailor deserved,
He was honoured to serve in the Royal Navy,
And to have sailed several times round the world,
So many moments in which he felt proud,
Especially when the Red Ensign was unfurled.

For us who mourned his last journey,
It was tinged with sadness and pain,
As our sailor weighed anchor for the last time,
And his face we saw once again,
And though we still miss him dearly,
With his warmth, and his generous style,
We can hold on to the treasured memory,
Of our sailor with his genial smile.

Written as a tribute to my dearly loved Brother-in-Law David Edward Hills (Dave) who departed this world on 11th July 2011 and is still always sadly missed by us his family.

'I Will Seek You There'

Wherever you are,
However near or far,
I will seek you there.

In the morning when you rise,
Dust the sleep from your eyes,
I will seek you there.

As the sun yields to the night,
And the darkness steals the light,
I will seek you there.

If you're anxious and alone,
And you think you're on your own,
I will seek you there.

As each brand-new day starts forth,
And you steer life's testing course,
I will seek you there.

When God's eternal light arrives,
To again entwine our lives,
When we are once more together,
In eternal peace forever,
I need no longer keep on seeking,
You'll be back in my safe keeping.

I'll be forever with you there.

Lord You're in Our Hearts

God our Father, Lord Deliverer,
Gave us the gift of life and light,
Through the light, through the darkness,
You're in our hearts each day and night.

God our Father, Lord of Goodness,
In the darkness you gave us sight,
Sent your Son for our salvation,
You're in our hearts each day and night.

God our Father, Lord of peace,
Your Son urged nations not to fight,
His teaching now so much unheeded,
You're in our hearts each day and night.

God our Father, Lord of compassion,
Shine on the world your eternal light,
We'll always be your faithful followers,
You're in our hearts each day and night.

God our Father, Lord Deliverer,
Thank you for the gift of life and light,
You always guide us through the darkness,
You're in our hearts each day and night.

The Mothers and Children of War Zones

When God looks down from heaven on high,
On the earth he made, he must ask himself why?
Some men he created have a terrible flaw,
Their greatest desire seems to be going to war.

No one is safe from the terrible destructions,
Violence seems to escalate from minor ructions,
Long standing feuds fuelled by prejudice and hate,
Spreading through generations, reconciliation too late.

Innocent children, maimed and killed,
Have no understanding why their blood's being spilled,
Cities and towns, embroiled in warfare's dark trouble,
Blitzed from the air, their homes razed to rubble.

Can God understand why this is done in his name?
He never wanted his people to kill or to maim,
They've created religious fervour he can't recognise,
Suddenly Friends and neighbours, they each despise.

Other Nations look on whilst these wars keep on raging,
During peace talks which are supposedly staging,
Dangerous factions fuel wars, whilst remaining unseen,
Spreading hatred like illness with no remedial vaccine.

Who knows where the wars and conflicts are heading,
Right now it appears through the world they're spreading,
Terrorism, destruction shows no sign of abating,
Using bullets and bombs instead of peaceful debating.

The Mothers and Children of War Zones....

One common factor seems apparent in all these ills,
Men are responsible for much of the terrorism that kills,
Maybe if women took over running the world,
Flags of peace and love would be globally unfurled.

We see many women tending wounds and broken bones,
So many exhausted but striving to salvage their homes,
We see women and children, terrified by air raid alarms,
And too often mothers, children dying in their arms.

Will there ever be an end to this wanton destruction?
The rape, the hatred, much wilful destruction,
Millions displaced at massive human cost!
Will it ever stop? It seems unlikely! Is peace really lost?

I wrote this in 2016 after watching on television, the people of Syria being killed by an uncaring President Assad, aided by an equally despotic Russian Ruler, and nothing changes as we witness in 2022 the Russian attacks on Ukraine.

Since adding to these footnotes, Ukraine is still suffering dreadful attacks from Russia We now have to watch the war involving Israel and Hamas, with collateral slaughter innocents on both sides. Yet unable to do anything to stop this madness!

Our Lady of Lourdes

Our Lady of Lourdes may I walk with you
When I'm feeling all alone?
May I come to you when I think I'm lost
And very far from home?
May I speak with you on the shoreline,
When I'm walking on the sand?
May I pray to you when my spirits are low,
And I seek a guiding hand?

Our Lady of Lourdes will you hear me,
When I ask for your redeeming love?
Will you help me to find solace?
And blessings from God above?
Will you find me midst the masses
Of deserving, praying nations?
Will you think me often wanting
With unreasonable expectations?

Our Lady of Lourdes if I seek reflection
May I find it at your holy shrine?
When I ask for understanding
Will forgiveness be truly mine?
When others need compassion
Will you feel I play my part?
When I kneel in prayer before you
Will you feel my aching heart?

Our Lady of Lourdes....

Our Lady of Lourdes when I bare my soul,
Will you see my human frailty?
When I pray to you, will I receive your love?
Through my life and for all eternity?
When I dwell within your chapel
Will I feel your tender care?
When I seek your sacred blessing,
You'll always hear my prayer.

All Alone at Christmas

Christmas time for Annie, no longer
Held the joy it used to bring,
When she would entertain her friends
With carols they'd love to sing,
But Annie was alone and elderly,
In a world seeming not to care,
Christmas goodwill messages all around,
But there appeared little charity to spare.

Of course Annie wasn't always old,
Having pursued a dedicated career,
A nurse, caring for the sick,
The work she held so very dear,
But retiring with an injured spine,
Her career was prematurely ended,
As her life became a trial,
And misfortune gradually descended.

Her husband died when he was young,
And Annie didn't marry again,
She didn't have any children and
Her brother had moved to Spain,
Immobile from her injured back
And the effects of being elderly,
Annie was all alone at home,
Valiantly coping with her infirmity.

All Alone at Christmas....

The worst affects of her loneliness made
Annie reflect on the sad times she'd had,
Christmas being the worst of all
When Annie was feeling alone and sad,
She would sit at her front room window,
On many a lonely Christmas morn,
Watching children enjoying their new bikes
Made her feel quite forlorn.

Bright sparkling lights on Christmas Day
Did nothing to lighten her mood,
Annie imagined nearby families
Preparing their Christmas food,
She looked at her small chicken
Which she had ready to be cooked,
And saw the small Christmas pudding
That she'd nearly overlooked.

The only company she had at Christmas
Her small radio and her TV,
She would receive no yuletide visitors,
In fact no other person would she see,
Annie of course was not unique,
For many elderly are lonely and alone,
Especially true at Christmas time,
In the sad confinement of their home.

All Alone at Christmas....

One Christmas day Annie sat in her chair,
Having not been feeling well,
She had a dreadful foreboding
As pain in her chest continued to swell,
Her experience told her that the pain
Was possibly her heart beginning to fail,
And as she tried to reach for her phone,
She fell back, knowing she was too frail.

It took many days for neighbours to realise
That Annie had not been seen,
Eventually they looked through her window,
She looked asleep, peaceful and serene,
But sadly she had died on Christmas Day,
That time when she was feeling so alone,
Whilst everyone was celebrating Christmas
Annie had sadly passed away on her own.

If you live near someone like Annie,
Try not to forget that they're all alone,
You could pop in and check that they're alright,
Remember they are confined within their home,
You may bring a true meaning of Christmas,
In an incredible and special way,
To someone feeling alone and forgotten,
And make them a truly memorable, Christmas Day.

As the Blossom Fills the Boughs

As the blossom fills the boughs,
Then you will blossom too,
Battling hard against the odds
Is what we knew you'd do.

None of us could ever guess
What trials before you lay,
At home amidst such loving care
Is where you now can stay.

We send wishes for you to keep improving,
With every passing hour,
As from your window, summer arrives,
With each new emerging flower.

Given time and with your inner strength,
You'll feel the fight has been worthwhile,
Though it's tough right now, we hope at times,
You'll still feel able to smile.

Dedicated to a friend as she managed to survive a massive stroke and is fighting to try to recover from the dreadful effects.

Rest Now Our Precious Son

Rest now in heaven's eternal peace
Our very precious Son,
Valiantly you fought to stay,
But we know that God has won,
Now left behind are grieving hearts
And sadness very deep,
With outpouring of the pain we feel,
We hurt, we sadly weep.

Take with you on that final journey,
All the love that we can give,
Our blessings for you, our precious Son,
And the life you managed to live,
Though your life's cut short,
You gave much love,
When far away and near,
Treasured memories of a wonderful Son,
Whose life we hold so very dear.

One day we will be together again
In God's amazing place of peace,
Where no wars will rage, all anger spent,
Human sufferings finally cease,
Till our souls are reunited again
And for us all life's final release,
We stand and mourn your last journey,
God bless you Andrew; rest in peace

I wrote this poem as a tribute to Andrew an ex Royal Marine, son of Janet & Malcolm King, who died November 2018 at only 53 having fought to try and survive from an aggressive brain tumour.

No Chance to Say Goodbye

We didn't get chance to say goodbye,
I couldn't hold you close; I didn't know you'd die,
Now you're gone and there's an empty space
In my heart aching to once more see your face.

Everywhere I look it feels like you're still here,
But reality clicks in and sadly it's clear
You're now gone and I'm here all alone,
It's strange without you, here in our home.

At night when I turn out the light, trying to sleep,
I reach for your warmth and then gently weep,
For you're not there, and we're so far apart,
I lay seeking solace, to mend my broken heart.

I know they say time heals, well so far it's not true,
For life feels very empty, as I no longer have you,
Our faith is strong and one day we'll reunite,
In everlasting peace, where I can forever hold you tight.

Until that day comes I will cherish the thought,
How much happiness and love living with you brought,
I will always want you here by my side,
The sorrow that you're not, I'll do my best now to hide.

I wrote this poem as a tribute to John Breen for his wife Pat. John sadly passed away May 2020. He was such a lovely, generous man.

Thank You Wherever You Are

Thank you for each day you make,
Thank you for each day I wake,
Thank you for each breath I take,
Thank you in your own name's sake.

Thank you for comfort when I am low,
Thank you for showing me the way to go,
Thank you for giving me the will to survive,
Thank you for helping me to feel so alive,

Thank you for the beauty of your earth,
Thank you for giving me the wonder of birth,
Thank you for the knowledge I've managed to unearth,
Thank you for showing me compassion and worth.

Thank you for everything, wherever you are,
Thank you though sometimes you seem so afar,
Thank you for guidance through my crises and strife,
Thank you for the gift of this wonderful life,
Thank You Wherever You Are.

The Little Angels of Aberfan

The innocent little Angels of Aberfan,
Who were lost in nineteen sixty six,
Had little chance of surviving that day,
A black and deadly, toxic mix,
The mining spoil set on a lethal course,
Caused by days of heavy rain,
Engulfing Pantglas junior school,
Inflicting death dealing horror and pain.

At nine thirteen, twenty first October,
Time stopped in this small valley town,
Death disguised as harmless waste,
From abandoned coal mine tips slid down,
There were many frantic efforts,
All were desperate. All in vain,
With so many trapped inside the school,
Never to return home again.

Now the survivors of the disaster,
Which gave Aberfan worldwide fame,
Have to live overlooking the tiny graves,
Constant reminders of their pain,
Each child denied the life they deserved,
To achieve adulthood as woman or man,
They'll remain forever in people's hearts,
Those innocent little Angels of Aberfan.

The Loving Life We Both Have Shared

The loving life we both have shared
Has finally come to a close,
Your life was taken prematurely,
And you are now in sad repose,
We can no longer walk together,
As we used to, hand in hand,
We can no longer sit in fond embrace,
On the golden, sun kissed sand.

I speak to the majestic mountains,
That from our garden I can see,
And say each day, how much I long,
For you to still be here with me,
I yearn for your smile, your loving kiss,
Your sweet and gentle touch,
I'm now alone with just my thoughts,
And I miss you oh so much.

The life we've shared together has been,
More precious than riches or gold
So many good times we both enjoyed,
In memories beginning to unfold,
There were problems, we saw them through,
Right through to their final end,
It was reassuring for me to know,
On you I could always depend.

The Loving Life....

You'll be in my every waking thought,
And my dreams will be of you,
Each flower in the garden you lovingly tended,
Will be a lasting memory too,
Of the loving wife with whom I had,
To share our happiness and pain,
Rest in eternal peace my love,
Until once more we're together again.

I wrote this poem for a dear friend who tragically lost his wife as a result of an unrelenting brain tumour and for whom I wrote my poem 'Weep Not for Me' page 77

They Never Came Home

Through the years they have no gain,
They strive to win in battles game,
But bound within the walls of pain,
They will but strive and strive again.

The ground now clears of former scene,
The air still holds what here hath been,
Man's glorious hour now dying lay,
Like summers end 'tis their last day.

No more to fight their battle's done,
Who is to count who lost, who won,
They strove to win that battle's fame,
They fight no more, none now remain.

The earth provides the heroes' bed,
There sleep our glorious sons now dead,
They do not share our painful grief,
For them no pain, just death's relief.

In memory of my Grandfather Arthur Straw. He did come home. He died soon after from a mortal wound and the effects of mustard gas. We never had the chance to know each other.

A Sadly Missed Friend

O dear friend, the many miles we spent walking,
The silly banter, boyhood humour, we never stopped talking,
Happy days in the Peaks of our beloved Derbyshire County,
Treasured moments worth more than any golden bounty,

You were always such a pleasure to spend the days with,
We were always so grateful for the biscuits you'd give,
The selection you'd bring, always brightened the day,
And your generosity resulted in you giving them away.

Though slightness of build, you had such a big heart,
Of our walking group you were the major part,
From a chance meeting quite some years ago,
We recruited more friends, our group started to grow.

Your easy going nature, kindness of spirit and a smile,
We've missed, for what seems like, quite some while,
Sadly you're no longer with us walking each dale and hill,
But we know, somewhere, you'll be smiling down on us still.

I wrote this poem in memory of a dear friend, Alan Braithwaite, who was such a kind and warm hearted person and we, his friends in our walking group, miss him greatly.

As I Stood at the Gates of Heaven

As I stood at the gates of Heaven,
And turned to say good bye,
I wanted to come and hold you,
When I saw you'd started to cry,
But the brightness there before me,
And the many beckoning hands,
Held me from coming back against,
Time's forward moving sands.

I hadn't planned for you to be alone,
But of course I had no say,
In when I was to leave this life,
And had to finally go away,
But you gave me all I could ever want,
That most precious gift of love,
And in return I'll watch over you,
From this special place above.

Please don't be sad thinking what we've lost,
But rejoice in what we've shared,
Reflect on our wonderful life together,
How much for each other we've cared,
And eventually in our glorious reunion,
When we're able to embrace each other again,
Eternally united in each other's arms,
No more tears, no more sadness, no more pain.

Please Stay With Me Through the Night

When I am in trouble I know you are there,
To help me find solace and fend off despair,
In the darkness when there seems to be little light,
Then I ask you please stay with me through the night.

When sometimes I'm anxious and fear things are wrong,
And I'm feeling weary and the road seems so long,
I seek the way home but it looks out of sight,
Then I ask you please stay with me through the night.

If family or friends may be encountering woe,
It's important for them to be certain to know,
If they seek your guidance I'm sure things will be alright,
Then I ask you please stay with them through the night.

The End of a Journey

This book has been a journey, and it's now coming to an end,
I'm hoping to the reader, a sincere message it will send,
Despite times of sadness, occurring in one's life,
I pray happiness is dominant, chasing away blues and strife.

I enjoy using words, I arrange into rhyme,
I get random ideas which occur any time,
In fact spontaneous thoughts, during night or day,
Composing new poems, creative ideas to convey.

It was at school I first engaged, with poetry and verse,
Discovering classic poets in whose poems I'd immerse,
I've many of their poetry books, most of which I've read,
Now it occurs to me that most of them are dead!

I'm aiming to still be around when you're reading my book,
I've tried to keep fit and healthy, but old age is mostly luck,
Therefore the title of this poem is intended for this tome,
I'm hopeful as you read it, my maker's not yet called me home.

Thank you for reading my poems

Best wishes

Rod Straw

Epilogue

If you have got this far through the book, a huge thank you, especially as the proceeds from the book will be donated to Muscular Dystrophy.

I recognise poetry is not to everyone's taste, rather like classical music or Marmite. However, if I or someone else talked you into buying it, and you didn't enjoy it, try selling it and if you feel so inclined donate the money to a charity of your choice.

It's unlikely I will write another poetry book, but I will always keep writing poems and who knows, having just reached the age of seventy seven, the decision on how long I'm around, is most definitely out of my hands.

As a final thought, I keep watching Bob Ross on TV who, bless him, died in 1995. As a prolific and inspiring American artist, I find his technique so absorbing, and I have in mind to paint a seascape, so the poetry production may have to wait for a while.

In the words of another influential man, Irish comedian, Dave Allen, "May your God go with you".

Best wishes & thank you